Celebrating Women

A COLLECTION OF INSIGHTFUL THOUGHTS

By Diane Voreis
and
Cheryl Henderson

Cover Illustration by Design Dynamics
Typography by MarketForce, Burr Ridge, IL

Published by Great Quotations Publishing Co.,
Glendale Heights, IL
Library of Congress Catalog Number: 98-71845
ISBN 1-56245-348-3

Printed in Hong Kong

*I*nside these pages is a legacy rich with insight and wisdom shared by women throughout the ages. This book is dedicated to women everywhere who use their talents to inspire, to nurture and to create a better world for all of us.

*The events in our lives happen
in a sequence in time
but in their significance to ourselves
they find their own order...
the continuous thread of revelation.*

-Eudora Welty

Challenges make you discover things about yourself that you never really knew. They're what make the instrument stretch— what make you go beyond the norm.

—Cicely Tyson

*Joy seems to me a step beyond happiness—
happiness is a sort of atmosphere
you can live in sometimes when you're lucky.
Joy is a light that fills you with hope
and faith and love.*

-Adela Rogers St. Johns

*L*ife is the first gift,
   love is the second
and understanding the third.

-Marge Piercy

There are two ways of spreading light:
to be the candle
or the mirror that reflects it.

-Edith Wharton

Invest in the human soul.
Who knows,
it might be a diamond in the rough.

-Mary McLeod Bethune

There is a fountain of youth:
it is your mind, your talents, the creativity
you bring to your life and the lives of people you love.
When you learn to tap this source,
you will have truly defeated age.

-Sophia Loren

$\mathcal{N}$ever get so fascinated
by the extraordinary
that you forget the ordinary.

-Magdalen Nabb

*It does not matter whether one paints a picture,
writes a poem, or carves a statue,
simplicity is the mark of a master-hand.
Don't run away with the idea that it is easy to cook
simply. It requires a long apprenticeship.*

-Elsie De Wolfe

*A people's literature is the great textbook
for real knowledge of them.
The writings of the day show the quality of the people
as no historical reconstruction can.*

-Edith Hamilton

You cannot hope to build a better world without improving the individuals. To that end each of us must work for his own improvement, and at the same time share a general responsibility for all humanity, our particular duty being to aid those to whom we think we can be most useful.

-Marie Curie

*The way of progress
is neither swift nor easy.*

-Marie Curie

*If love does not know how to give and take
without restrictions, is not love,
but a transaction that never fails
to lay stress on a plus and a minus.*

-Emma Goldman

$\mathcal{L}$et the world know you as you are,
not as you think you should be,
because sooner or later, if you are posing,
you will forget the pose, and then where are you?

-Fannie Brice

*W*hen you get into a tight place
and it seems you can't go on, hold on,
for that's the place and time that the tide will turn.

-Harriet Beecher Stowe

*E*njoy life for at least one year.
Do not take on any new
and perplexing problems.

-Eleanor Roosevelt

$\mathcal{B}$attles in life are never won. I mean, you don't have your household budget permanently balanced; you have to balance it every year. Life's a continuous business, and so is success and requires continuous effort.

-Margaret Thatcher

If you want anything said, ask a man.
If you want anything done, ask a woman.
-Margaret Thatcher

You may have to fight a battle
more than once to win it.
-Margaret Thatcher

To be somebody,
a woman does not have to be more like a man,
but has to be more of a woman.

-Dr. Sally E. Shaywitz

*Trouble is a sieve
through which we sift our acquaintances.
Those too big to pass through
are our friends.*

-Arlene Francis

Life begets life.
Energy creates energy.
It is by spending oneself
that one becomes rich.

-Sarah Bernhardt

*M*istakes are a fact of life.
It is the response to error
that counts.

-Nikki Giovanni

The one thing that doesn't abide majority rule
is a person's conscience.

-Harper Lee

It's the friends that you can call up at 4 a.m. that matter.

-Marlene Dietrich

Your luck is how you treat people.

-Bridget O'Donnell

For fast-acting relief,
try slowing down.

-Lily Tomlin

*We can do no great things-
only small things with great love.*
    -Mother Teresa

The fruit of love is service.

The fruit of service is peace.

And peace begins with a smile.
    -Mother Teresa

Minister the same measure
of grace and loving kindness
to the mighty and the lowly.

-Mother Teresa

ope is the thing with feathers,
that perches in the soul,
and sings the tune without the words,
and never stops at all.

-Emily Dickinson

Remember, Ginger Rogers did everything Fred Astaire did, but she did it backwards and in high heels.

—Faith Whittlesey

 *think that education is power.
I think that being able to communicate
with people is power. One of my main goals on
the planet is to encourage people to
empower themselves.*

-Oprah Winfrey

*Far away there in the sunshine
are my highest aspirations. I may not
reach them, but I can look up and see their beauty,
believe in them and try to follow where they lead.*

-Louisa May Alcott

Character contributes to beauty.
It fortifies a woman as her youth fades.
A mode of conduct, a standard of courage, discipline,
fortitude and integrity can do a great deal
to make a woman beautiful.

-Jacqueline Bisset

*It's so clear that you have to cherish everyone.
I think that's what I get from these older black
women, that every soul is to be cherished,
that every flower is to bloom.*

-Alice Walker

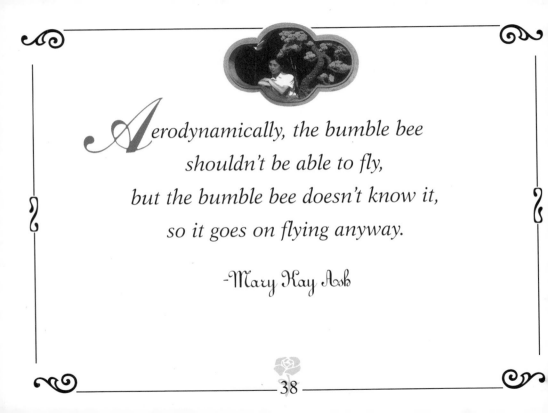

Aerodynamically, the bumble bee
shouldn't be able to fly,
but the bumble bee doesn't know it,
so it goes on flying anyway.

-Mary Kay Ash

*Getting ahead in a difficult profession
requires avid faith in yourself.
That is why some people with mediocre talent,
but with great inner drive,
go much further than people
with vastly superior talent.*

—Sophia Loren

*If you approach each new person you meet
in a spirit of adventure, you will find yourself endlessly
fascinated by the new channels of thought and experience
and personality that you encounter. I do not mean
simply the famous people of the world,
but the people from every walk and condition of life.*

-Eleanor Roosevelt

*Truly being needed gives an exhilaration,
energy and strength like nothing else.*

—Eleanor Roosevelt

*All human beings have failings —
needs that lead to stress, and stress that leads to
temptations.*

—Eleanor Roosevelt

*God sent children for another purpose
than merely to keep up the race—to enlarge our hearts;
and to make us unselfish and full of kindly sympathies
and affections; to give our souls higher aims; to call out
all our faculties to extended enterprise and exertion;
and to bring round our firesides bright faces,
happy smiles and loving, tender hearts.*

-Mary Botham Howitt

*pray that I may be all that
my mother would have been
had she lived in an age
when women could aspire and achieve,
and daughters are cherished as much as sons.*

-Justice Ruth Bader Ginsburg

Life is the only real counselor;
wisdom unfiltered through personal experience
does not become a part of the moral tissue.

-Edith Wharton

*It is the personality of the mistress
that the home expresses.
Men are forever guests in our homes,
no matter how much happiness they may find there.*

-Elsie De Wolfe

Love is something like the clouds that were in the sky before the sun came out. You cannot touch the clouds, you know; but you feel the rain and know how glad the flowers and the thirsty earth are to have it after a hot day. You cannot touch love either; but you feel the sweetness that it pours into everything.

-Annie Sullivan

I have a simple philosophy.
Fill what's empty.
Empty what's full.
And scratch what itches.

-Alice Roosevelt Longworth

Thoughts are energy
and you can make your world
or break your world
by your thinking.

-Susan L. Taylor

*earn to get in touch with silence within yourself
and know that everything in life has a purpose.
There are no mistakes, no coincidences;
all events are blessings given to us
to learn from.*

-Elizabeth Kubler-Ross

The universe is made up of stories,

not atoms.

-Muriel Rukeyser

ou need to claim the events of your life to make yourself yours. When you truly possess all you have been and done, which may take some time, you are fierce with reality.

-Florida Scott Maxwell

*A kiss is a lovely trick designed by nature
to stop speech when words become superfluous.*

-Ingrid Bergman

*Civility costs nothing
and buys everything.*

- Lady Mary Wortley Montague

At the end of your life, you will never regret not having passed one more test, not winning one more verdict or not closing one more deal. You will regret time not spent with a husband, a friend, a child or a parent.

—Barbara Bush

*The real art of conversation
is not only to say the right thing at the right place,
but to leave unsaid the wrong thing
at the tempting moment.*

-Lady Dorothy Nevill

I believe you rarely achieve
more than you expect.

—Carol Grosse

*A #2 pencil and a dream
can take you anywhere.*

-Joyce A. Myers

There are people who put their dreams in a little box and say, "Yes, I've got dreams, of course, I've got dreams." Then they put the box away and bring it out once in awhile to look in it, and yep, they're still there. There are great dreams, but they never even get out of the box. It takes an uncommon amount of guts to put your dreams on the line, to hold them up and say, "How good or how bad am I?" That's where courage comes in.

-Erma Bombeck

*The only place you find
success before work is in the dictionary.*

-May V. Smith

*Whenever I have to choose between two evils,
I always like to try the one
I haven't tried before.*

-Mae West

The secret of joy is contained in one word—
excellence. To know how to do
something well is to enjoy it.

-Pearl S. Buck

*Prejudices, it is well known,
are most difficult to eradicate from the heart
whose soil has never been loosened
or fertilized by education;
they grow there, firm as weeds among rocks.*

–Charlotte Bronte

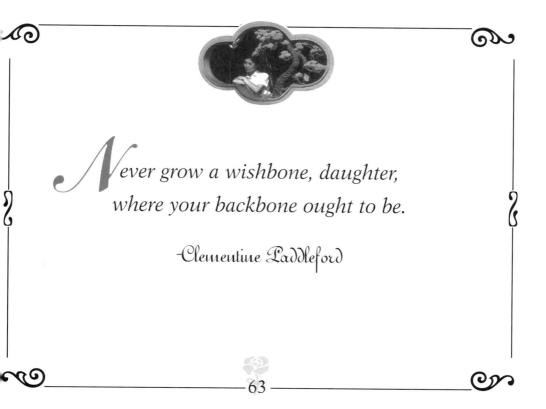

*ever grow a wishbone, daughter,
where your backbone ought to be.*

-Clementine Paddleford

'Tis easy enough to be pleasant,
when life flows like a song.
But the man worthwhile is the one who will smile
when everything goes dead wrong.

-Ella Wheeler Wilcox

*If you don't like the way the world is,
you change it.
You have an obligation to change it.
You just do it one step at a time.*

-Marian Wright Edelman

*The especial genius of women
I believe to be electrical in movement,
intuitive in function, spiritual in tendency.*

-Margaret Fuller

I *believe that what woman resents*
is not so much giving herself in pieces
as giving herself purposelessly.

-Anne Morrow Lindbergh

Security is mostly a superstition. It does not exist in nature, nor do the children of men as a whole experience it. Avoiding danger is no safer in the long run than outright exposure. Life is either a daring adventure or nothing.

-Helen Keller

Everything has its wonders,
even darkness and silence,
and I learn, whatever state I may be in,
therein to be content.

-Helen Keller

...One is taught by experience
to put a premium on those few people
who can appreciate you for what you are...

-Gail Godwin

*It is always wise to stop wishing for things
long enough to enjoy the fragrances
of those now flowering.*

-Patrice Gifford

$\mathscr{A}$fter an acquaintance of ten minutes
many women will exchange confidences
that a man would not reveal
to a lifelong friend.

-Page Smith

*T*here is no pleasure in having nothing to do;
the fun is in having lots to do
and not doing it.

-Mary Little

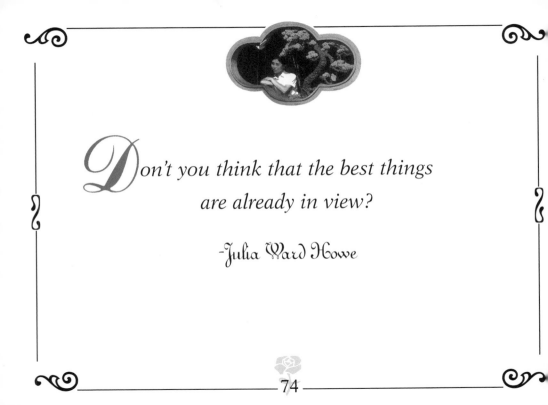

*Don't you think that the best things
are already in view?*

-Julia Ward Howe

A master can tell you
what he expects of you.
A teacher, though, awakens your own expectations.

-Patricia Neal

Men are taught to apologize
for their weaknesses,
women for their strengths.

-Lois Wyse

The cure for anything is salt water—
sweat, tears or the sea.

-Isak Dinesen

$\mathcal{M}$y mother drew a distinction between achievement and success. She said that achievement is the knowledge that you have studied and worked hard and done the best that is in you. Success is being praised by others, and that's nice, too, but not as important or satisfying. Always aim for achievement and forget about success.

-Helen Hayes

*D*on't compromise yourself.
You are all you've got.

-Betty Ford

Life is to be lived.
If you have to support yourself,
you had bloody well better find some way
that is going to be interesting.
And you don't do that by sitting around
wondering about yourself.

-Katherine Hepburn

Without discipline, there is no life at all.

-Katherine Hepburn

*If you obey all the rules
you miss all the fun.*

-Katherine Hepburn

*If one is lucky,
a solitary fantasy can totally transform
one million realities.*

-Maya Angelou

$\mathcal{B}$eauty has nothing to do with possession.
If possession and beauty must go together, then we are
lost souls. A beautiful flower is not to be possessed,
it's there to be beheld. You're not going to take a beautiful
painting off the museum wall. It's there for your pleasure.

–Diana Vreeland

*Success in the modern world
takes far more than knowledge.
It takes stability, stamina, level-headedness, courage,
a desire to learn and an ability to
make good use of one's learning.*

-Alice L. Dement

*You don't manage people;
you manage things.
You lead people.*

-Admiral Grace Hooper

If you seek to be understood,
then dedicate your life to understanding others.
If you seek to be comforted,
then dedicate yourself to giving comfort.
If you seek a greater faith,
then commit yourself to planting it in others.

-Sue Monk Kidd

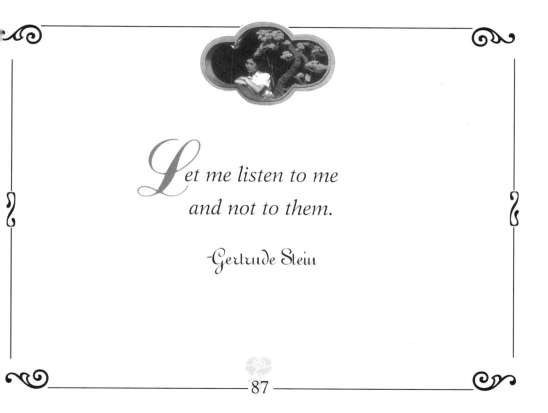

*et me listen to me
and not to them.*

-Gertrude Stein

$\mathcal{I}$f you want a place in the sun,
you've got to put up with a few blisters.

-Abigail Van Buren

*If we are to achieve a richer culture,
rich in contrasting values, we must
recognize the whole gamut of human potentialities,
and so weave a less arbitrary social fabric,
one in which each diverse human gift
will find a fitting place.*

-Margaret Mead

ake two homes for thyself, my daughter.
One actual home...
and the other a spiritual home,
which thou art to carry with thee always.

-Catherine of Sienna

*If we had no winter,
the spring would not be so pleasant;
if we did not sometimes taste of adversity,
prosperity would not be so welcome.*

-Anne Bradstreet

It had long since come to my attention that people of accomplishment rarely sat back and let things happen to them. They went out and happened to things.

-Elinor Smith

Women share with men the need for personal success, even the taste for power, and no longer are we willing to satisfy those needs through the achievements of surrogates, whether husbands, children or merely role models.

-Elizabeth Dole

If the world seems cold to you,
kindle fires to warm it.

-Lucy Larcom

Courageous risks are life-giving,
help you grow, make you brave
and better than you think you are.

-Joan L. Curcio

*T*rees are not known by their leaves,
not even by their blossoms,
but by their fruits.

-Eleanor of Aquitaine

To have ideas is to gather flowers;
to think is to weave them into garlands.

-Anne Sophie Swetchine

The past is a cancelled check.
Your only legal tender is now.

–Rita Davenport

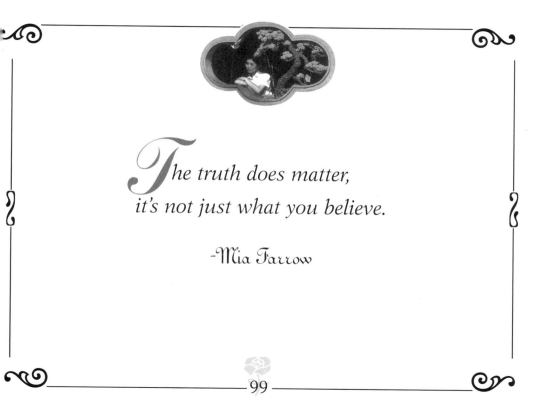

The truth does matter,
it's not just what you believe.

-Mia Farrow

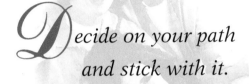

*$\mathcal{D}$ecide on your path
and stick with it.*

-Phyllis Hyman

*D*on't give up,
   don't ever give up,
  because without pain there cannot be joy,
and both are what make us know we are alive.

-Gloria Vanderbilt

*T*oo many people
let others stand in their way
and don't go back for one more try.

-Rosabeth Moss Kanter

To stay ahead,
always have your next idea
waiting in the wings.

-Rosabeth Moss Kanter

*In soloing—as in other activities—
it is far easier to start something
than it is to finish it.*

-Amelia Earhart

I've never banked on luck
and I'm afraid of people who do.
Luck is recognizing opportunity.

-Lucille Ball

*There are no hopeless situations;
there are only men and women
who have grown hopeless.*

-Clare Boothe Luce

*No one should weigh love
against expediency.*

-Trude Lash

*My favorite law of physics:
a body in motion
tends to stay in motion.*

-Melissa Seaman

I can do that.

-Gracie Allen

The trouble with the rat race
is that if you win,
you're still a rat.

-Lily Tomlin

*To me laughter is the finest sound there is.
It is the sound of the human spirit,
all that is best about life.*

-Linda Ellerbee

I f the ends bring me out wrong,
ten angels swearing I was right
would make no difference.

-Janet Reno

*It's what you are inside
that matters. You yourself are your
only real capital.*

-Gloria Vanderbilt

*The power
is in the consistency.*

-Gloria Copeland

*You can't shake hands
with a clenched fist.*

-Golda Meir

Release anger and take steps toward compassion and forgiveness.

-Jean Borysenko

*H*ell is not pain and fire,
but boredom.

-Joan Rivers

*You gravitate towards
what you think about the most.*

-Rita Davenport

*$\mathcal{F}$ight for what you believe in
even though you may not have supporters.*

-Shirley Chisholm

*R*espect and love your parents;
it nurtures your heart.

-Erma Bolden

*Humor has a way of washing away
the emotional toxins from the mind,
lifting the spirit and providing a new
perspective to life's problems.*

-Anne Frahm

*D*on't wear your sex
like a badge on your sleeve.

-Diane Feinstein

Sports is an excellent opportunity for girls to work as a team under every possible condition—winning, losing, happy, tired and grumpy. It forces them to deal with unpleasant emotions and get over it.

-Gabrielle Reece

Staying curious about what is going on around you often times is the best source of your opportunities.

-Susan Byrne

Everyone has a talent.
What is rare is the courage to follow the talent
to the dark place where it leads.

-Erica Jong

There are two things people want
more than sex and money...
Recognition and praise.

-Mary Kay Ash

*Each of us guards a gate of change
that can only be opened from inside.*

-Marilyn Ferguson

Being in love
with the idea of love
tends to cloud your vision.

-Phyllis Hyman

I

have always considered it a beautiful day
when I can stretch my body
with my face turned to the sun.

-Bloeme Eveis Emden
(holocaust survivor)

he future of women's rights
to a great extent rests with women.
Today, we are the majority of votes in most elections.

-Diane Feinstein

$\mathcal{G}$uided by conviction
a family can move through painful adversities
toward undreamed-of achievements.

-Doris Kerns Goodwin

If you have lost your joy
rekindle your relationship with God.

Cheryl Murray

*When you leave your comfort zone
is when you experience challenge and adventure.*

-Rita Davenport

*Creative solutions
are usually found during quiet moments.*

-Gunnie Clark

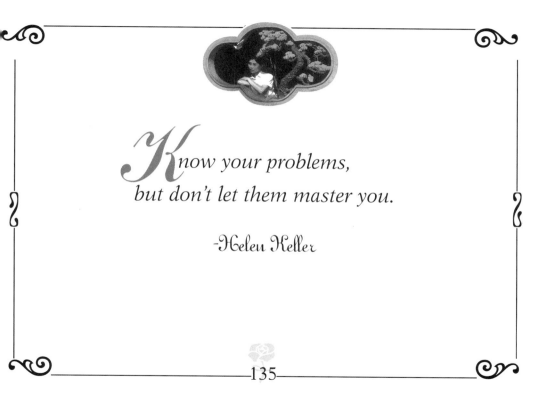

*K*now your problems,
but don't let them master you.

-Helen Keller

*Violence has become
the salt and pepper of our television -
always someone killing, but no one mourning.*

-Janet Reno

*The voice of conscience
is so delicate that it is easy to stifle,
but it is also clear that it is impossible to mistake it.*

-Madame de Stael

$\mathcal{L}$ife is like putting together a jigsaw puzzle.
In the beginning, it's a confusing jumble,
but as the pieces fall into place, a picture of who
you are and the goals that are important to you
begin to emerge.

-Cherie Calbou

*I*t is up to you—
use your common sense,
instincts, past experience,
present needs and future goals.

-Marilyn Diamond

*Helplessness and hopelessness
are just as lethal as
cigarettes and bullets.*

-Noreen Quillin

Who you love is what life is all about,
being there for people
who are important to you.

-Joan Rivers

*$\mathcal{W}$ith so much opportunity
to accomplish so many different things,
take the time to determine which challenge
is peculiarly suited for you.*

-Ester Lape

*Intellectually, I can see marriage
is just a piece of paper,
but not in my heart.*

-Mia Farrow

Make your own ladder of success.

-Gwen Willhite

*felt some jealousy that she had graduated,
and I was stuck, still trying to figure out
lessons about life.*

-Mary Fisher

***K**eep your face to the sunshine
and you won't notice the shadows.*

-Helen Keller

It is often interesting, in retrospect,
to consider the trifling causes that lead to great events.
A chance encounter, a thoughtless remark
that causes a tortuous chain reaction
to be set into motion.

-Patricia Moyes

*Loneliness and the feeling of being unwanted
is the most terrible poverty.*

-Mother Teresa

Perhaps it was meant simply as entertainment,
and no real lesson was intended,
but it certainly carries one.

-Eleanor Roosevelt

*We don't see things as they are,
we see things as we are.*

-Anais Nin

*The dream was always running ahead of one.
To catch up, to live for a moment in unison with it,
that was the miracle.*

-Anais Nin

It is the function of art to renew our perception. What we are familiar with we cease to see. The writer shakes up the familiar scene and, as if by magic, we see a new meaning in it.

-Anaïs Nin

*People of character
don't allow the environment
to dictate their style.*

-Lucille Kallen

152

Laugh out loud, resist fear,
take on a new challenge—
find out what life has to offer
by sticking out your neck.

-Gabrielle Reece

*The only thing I know about
is that love is all there is.*

-Emily Dickinson

Life is not about dates and times.

It is about an experience.

It is about acceptance.

It is about sinking below,

rising above, giving up and going on.

-Patti Labelle

$\mathcal{K}$indness is a language
which the deaf can hear,
and the blind can see.

-Heather Whitestone

*One should never consent
to creep when one feels an impulse to soar.*

-Helen Keller

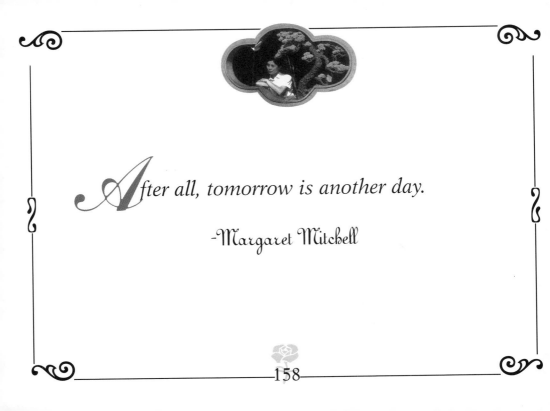

After all, tomorrow is another day.

-Margaret Mitchell

*L*ife is full of magical moments
and unanswered questions.

-Dolly Parton

Don't be satisfied with just one success.
Let every success be a springboard
to a new challenge.

-Oprah Winfrey

$\mathcal{I}$magination
has always had powers of resurrection
that no science can match.

-Ingrid Bengis

*T*here is nothing final about a mistake,
it's being taken as final.

-Phyllis Bottome

*Self-pity in its early stages
is as snug as a feather mattress.
Only when it hardens
does it become uncomfortable.*

-Maya Angelou

hen one door of happiness closes,
another opens, but often we look so long at the
closed door that we do not see the one
which has been opened for us.

-Helen Keller

If you think you can, you can.
And if you think you can't,
you're right.

-Mary Kay Ash

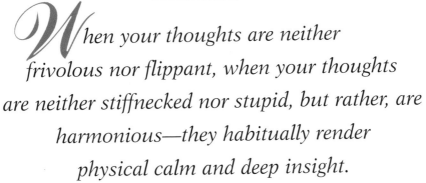

When your thoughts are neither frivolous nor flippant, when your thoughts are neither stiffnecked nor stupid, but rather, are harmonious—they habitually render physical calm and deep insight.

-Hildegarde of Bingen

*Sit down,
feel the wind and the sun,
hear the birds and smell the sea—
life has so many untold possibilities.*

-Linda Ellerbee

Other Titles by Great Quotations

301 Ways to Stay Young At Heart
African-American Wisdom
A Lifetime of Love
A Light Heart Lives Long
Angel-grams
As A Cat Thinketh
A Servant's Heart
Astrology for Cats
Astrology for Dogs
A Teacher is Better Than Two Books
A Touch of Friendship
Can We Talk
Celebrating Women
Chicken Soup
Chocoholic Reasonettes
Daddy & Me
Dare to Excel
Erasing My Sanity
Falling in Love
Fantastic Father, Dependable Dad
Golden Years, Golden Words
Graduation Is Just The Beginning
Grandma, I Love You
Happiness is Found Along The Way

High Anxieties
Hooked on Golf
I Didn't Do It
Ignorance is Bliss
I'm Not Over the Hill
Inspirations
Interior Design for Idiots
Let's Talk Decorating
Life's Lessons
Life's Simple Pleasures
Looking for Mr. Right
Midwest Wisdom
Mommy & Me
Mom's Homemade Jams
Mother, I Love You
Motivating Quotes for Motivated People
Mrs. Murphy's Laws
Mrs. Webster's Dictionary
My Daughter, My Special Friend
Only a Sister
Parenting 101
Pink Power
Read the Fine Print

Reflections
Romantic Rhapsody
Size Counts !
Social Disgraces
Sports Prose
Stress or Sanity
The ABC's of Parenting
The Be-Attitudes
The Birthday Astrologer
The Cornerstones of Success
The Rose Mystique
The Secret Language of Men
The Secret Language of Women
The Secrets in Your Face
The Secrets in Your Name
TeenAge of Insanity
Thanks from the Heart
The Lemonade Handbook
The Mother Load
The Other Species
Wedding Wonders
Words From The Coach
Working Woman's World

Great Quotations Publishing Company

1967 Quincy Court
Glendale Heights, IL 60139, U.S. A.
Phone: 630-582-2800   Fax: 630-582-2813
http: //www.greatquotations.com